P9-BYR-855

Monkeys

Anne Schreiber

NATIONAL
GEOGRAPHIC

Washington, D.C.

To Jacob, Sammy, and Noah—a barrel of monkeys!
—A. S.

The publisher and author gratefully acknowledge the review
of proofs for this book by Joe Knobbe of the Saint Louis Zoo and
Keith Lovett of the Palm Beach Zoo.

Copyright © 2013 National Geographic Society
Published by the National Geographic Society, Washington, D.C. 20036. All rights reserved.
Reproduction in whole or in part without written permission of the publisher is prohibited.

ISBN: 978-1-4263-1106-2 (Trade paper)
ISBN: 978-1-4263-1107-9 (Library)

Design by YAY! Design

Photo Credits
Cover, Elio Della Ferrera/naturepl.com; 1, Josh Brown/National Geographic My Shot; 2, Imagewerks Japan/Getty Images; 4-5, Brad Starry/National Geographic My Shot; 7 (UPLE), Pete Oxford/Minden Pictures; 7 (UPRT), Fiona Rogers/naturepl.com; 7 (LO), Chiangkunta/Flickr RM/Getty Images; 8, Thomas Marent/Minden Pictures/Corbis; 9, Danita Delimont/Alamy; 10-11, Marsel van Oosten/www.squiver.com; 13 (UPLE), Thomas Marent/Visuals Unlimited, Inc./Getty Images; 13 (UPRT), Judith Arsenault/National Geographic My Shot; 13 (LE CTR), Anup Shah/Corbis; 13 (RT CTR), Jennifer Kraft/National Geographic My Shot; 13 (LOLE), Dr. Clive Bromhall/Getty Images; 13 (LORT), Judith Arsenault/National Geographic My Shot; 14, Jerry Young/Dorling Kindersley; 15, Eric Isselée/Shutterstock; 16, Christianne Lagura/National Geographic Stock; 17, Thomas Marent/Minden Pictures/Corbis; 18, Donna Tramontozzi/National Geographic My Shot; 19, Bruno D'Amicis/naturepl.com; 20, Pete Oxford/Minden Pictures/Corbis; 22, SA Team/Foto Natura/Minden Pictures; 23, Pomchai Kittiwongsakul/AFP/Getty Images; 24 (UP), Mario Tizon/National Geographic My Shot; 24 (CTR), Cathleen Burnham/National Geographic My Shot; 24 (LO), AP Photo/Public Library of Science, Maurice Emetshu; 25 (UP), Anup Shah/Getty Images; 25 (CTR), Frank Lukasseck/Getty Images; 25 (LO), Mint Images-Frans Lanting/Getty Images; 26-27, Cyril Ruoso/JH Editorial/Minden Pictures/Corbis; 28, Mattias Klum/National Geographic Stock; 29, Barbara Walton/epa/Corbis; 30 (UP), Karl Ammann/Digital Vision; 30 (CTR), Matt Propert/National Geographic Society; 30 (LO), Jeremy Phan/National Geographic My Shot; 31 (UPLE), James Pelton/National Geographic My Shot; 31 (UPRT), Branislav Bieleny/National Geographic My Shot; 31 (LE CTR), M Rutherford/Shutterstock; 31 (RT CTR), Sebastien Barreau/National Geographic My Shot; 31 (LOLE), Andrey Pavlov/Shutterstock; 31 (LORT), Hakuei Huang/National Geographic My Shot; 32 (UPLE), Anna Kucherova/Shutterstock; 32 (UPRT), Jeff Mauritzen; 32 (LE CTR), Cyril Ruoso/JH Editorial/Minden Pictures/Corbis; 32 (RT CTR), Galyna Andrushko/Shutterstock; 32 (LOLE), worldswildlifewonders/Shutterstock; 32 (LORT), Dr. Clive Bromhall/Getty Images; art in running head, stock09/Shutterstock; art in "Monkey Talk" boxes, Brad Collett/Shutterstock.

Printed in the United States of America
13/WOR/2

Table of Contents

Monkey Business

Yellow baboons

Who spends their
days climbing in trees,
leaping up high or
swinging with ease?

Who calls out in
grunts, screeches,
or whoops?

Who lives together in
groups we call troops?

Monkeys, that's who!

Monkeying Around

Monkeys live in many different kinds of habitats. They live in jungles and on mountains. They live in rain forests, grasslands, and even in cities and towns.

Many monkeys are arboreal (ar–BOR–ee–ul) monkeys. That means they live in the trees. Other monkeys live mostly on the ground.

Monkey Talk

HABITAT: The place where a plant or animal lives in nature

Common marmoset

Gelada baboon

Macaque

Monkey Talk

CANOPY: The area high up in the trees

PREHENSILE: Made for grabbing hold, like some monkeys' tails

The spider monkey uses its strong, prehensile (pree-HEN-sil) tail to grab and hold on.

Life in the Trees

Many arboreal monkeys live in the canopy (KAN-uh-pee) layer of the trees. They move from branch to branch.

Why don't they fall? Some monkeys use their tails like a third arm. Other monkeys have pads on their bottoms to keep them in place.

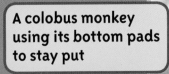

A colobus monkey using its bottom pads to stay put

9

Ah, the Spa!

Snow monkeys are macaques
(muh-KAKS). Many of them
live in the mountains of Japan.
These monkeys know how to
warm up in the winter.

Snow monkeys

They bathe in the hot mountain water. The water is heated inside the Earth and bubbles to the surface. Snow monkeys like to relax and play in the warm water.

All in the Family

Monkeys and apes are both primates (PRY-mates). Primates are animals known for their big brains. They are smart. Their eyes face straight ahead. Sound like someone you know?

Surprise! Humans are primates, too. Humans are in the ape family! Chimpanzees, bonobos, orangutans, gibbons, gorillas, and humans are all apes.

Monkey Talk

PRIMATE: An animal with forward-facing eyes, grasping hands or tail, and handlike feet

Apes | Monkeys

T A I L

do not have tails | have tails

B O D Y

usually larger, can walk on two legs | usually smaller, walk on four legs

B R A I N

very smart, most use tools | smart, most do not use tools

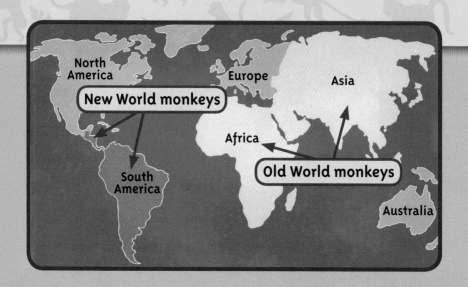

New World monkeys live in parts of Central and South America. They are small and have flat noses. They live in trees.

Capuchin monkeys live in parts of Central and South America.

Old World monkeys live in parts of Africa and Asia. They are larger, and their noses are not flat. They live in mountains, grasslands, forests, and towns. They sit on their bottom pads.

Vervet monkeys live in parts of Africa.

15

Monkey Babies

Monkey mothers have a strong bond with their babies. This bond helps babies learn from their mothers. Monkey babies stay close to their moms for the first year.

Monkey Talk

BOND: A strong feeling between animals that makes them close. Mother and baby monkeys have a strong bond.

Young macaque

Silvered leaf monkeys

A newborn monkey holds on tight to its mother's front. Later, it rides on its mom's back.

Baboons

Barbary macaques

Young monkeys play together. They wrestle and tumble. When boys are older, they usually go off to join another troop. Most girl monkeys stay with their moms. One day they will raise their own families.

Tools of the Trade

Brown capuchin

Q What do you get when you cross a jungle with an office?

A Monkey business.

Most monkeys don't use tools. But capuchin (KA-pyu-shen) monkeys do! They sometimes use tools to find food. They use rocks to dig up potatoes. They also use rocks to crack open nuts and seeds.

Rocks aren't the only tools these monkeys use. When capuchin monkeys need to protect themselves against snakes, they may use a tree branch as a club.

21

Want a Banana?

Do you have to eat your fruits and vegetables? Monkeys do, too!

Monkeys eat more than 200 different types of food.

Most monkeys eat plants such as seeds, leaves, and fruit, including bananas! Monkeys sometimes eat insects, too.

This Midas tamarin is eating seed pods.

Every year people in the city of Lopburi, Thailand, throw a party for the macaque monkeys that live there. People put out more than 4,000 pounds of food for the monkeys!

6 Marvelous Monkeys

Loudest!

Howler monkeys can be heard up to three miles away.

Tiniest!

The pygmy marmoset is the world's smallest monkey. It's about the size of a banana.

Newest Found!

The lesula monkey was just discovered in the Democratic Republic of the Congo in Africa.

Biggest!

A male mandrill can be three feet long. It weighs about 77 to 100 pounds. That's as big as a large dog.

Furriest!

Golden snub-nosed monkeys have thick fur to keep them warm. They live in the cold mountains of China.

Fastest!

Patas can run up to 35 miles an hour. That's as fast as a racehorse.

Friends and Family

Monkeys have strong bonds with the other members of their troop.

Grooming is the main way monkeys show they care. Mothers groom babies. Females groom other females. And couples groom each other.

Monkey Talk

GROOM: To clean, brush, and care for

Q Why did the monkey make new friends?

A He wanted to branch out.

Hanuman langurs

27

Monkeys in Trouble

What animal is the biggest danger to monkeys? Humans!

We have cut down forests where monkeys live. Without forests, monkeys have no place to go.

Forests that have been cut down in Malaysia

Proboscis (proh-BOS-is) monkeys live in the jungles of Borneo. Only a few thousand of them are left in the world. The mangrove forests they need for food are disappearing.

But some people are working to protect the land where monkeys live. This will help keep these amazing animals in our world.

Stump Your Parents

Can your parents answer these questions about monkeys? You might know more than they do!

Answers are at the bottom of page 31.

1

Where do monkeys live?

A. In cities
B. In forests
C. In jungles
D. All of the above

2

A monkey uses its prehensile tail to _____.

A. Fight
B. Sleep
C. Grab
D. Smell

Some monkeys are arboreal. Where do arboreal animals spend most of their time?

A. On the ground
B. In the air
C. In trees
D. Underwater

3

4 When a baby monkey is born, she
_____.

A. Stays in her mother's pouch
B. Clings to her mother's front
C. Hangs from her mother's tail
D. Can immediately climb trees

Which animals are primates?

A. Monkeys
B. Great apes
C. Humans
D. All of the above

5

6

What do monkeys eat?

A. Bananas
B. Insects
C. Seeds
D. All of the above

What is the main way that monkeys show they care for each other?

A. They jump up and down.
B. They climb together.
C. They groom each other.
D. They play board games.

7

BOND: A strong feeling between animals that makes them close. Mother and baby monkeys have a strong bond.

CANOPY: The area high up in the trees

GROOM: To clean, brush, and care for

HABITAT: The place where a plant or animal lives in nature

PREHENSILE: Made for grabbing hold, like some monkeys' tails

PRIMATE: An animal with forward-facing eyes, grasping hands or tail, and handlike feet